From the Heart

...a fine compliment to ***Together for Life***...any priest preparing an engaged couple for marriage would find this a helpful tool.

—National Association of Catholic Family Life Ministers

From the Heart

Personalizing
Your Wedding Homily
with Your Own
Hopes and Expectations

Joseph M. Champlin

International Standard Book Number: 0-87793-647-1

Cover and text design by Brian C. Conley

Photos: Cleo Photography, 12, 30, 36
         Jim Whitmer, 16, 20

Printed and bound in the United States of America.

Library of Congress Cataloging-in-Publication Data

Champlin, Joseph M.
   From the heart : personalizing your wedding homily with your own hopes and expectations / Joseph M. Champlin.
       p.   cm.
     Includes bibliographical references.
     ISBN 0-87793-647-1
     1. Marriage—Religious aspects—Catholic Church.   2. Marriage
service.   3. Catholic Church—Liturgy—Texts.   I. Title.
BX2250.C48   1998
251'.1—dc21   97-35413
                                                                   CIP

Contents

Part I

Composing Your Hopes and Expectations

The two of you have, by this time, probably arranged most of the details for your wedding service in church.

No doubt your goal has been to plan a nuptial ceremony that will be comfortable and yet distinctive. It will observe a familiar pattern which all the guests can clearly recognize and easily follow. At the same time, it will contain elements that reflect your uniqueness as individual persons and, consequently, your specialness as a couple.

The Catholic church wants to encourage and help brides and grooms to accomplish this ideal. It provides you with a rich treasury of readings and prayers, formulas and blessings, symbols and gestures to choose from. It urges you to select those which best express your present love and future dreams.

Nearly eight million couples have already done what you are in the midst of doing. They have looked at the many options that the *Rite of Marriage* provides and, using *Together for Life*, have developed wedding celebrations that were both familiar and unique.

This booklet describes and illustrates an additional possibility that can further personalize your wedding celebration. As you will note from the examples which follow, that option is simple, but quite creative. Moreover, its use can prove to be a very powerful and deeply moving experience.

The alternative suggested in this booklet, however, must be a venture that enjoys both your mutual approval and the presiding clergy's cooperative consent.

It works in this way:

Shortly before the wedding each of you writes out, somewhat briefly, your hopes and expectations for the marriage. You do so separately and without showing those compositions to one another. At the rehearsal you present them to the priest or deacon. He in turn weaves those words into his homily, blending your thoughts with his own reflections on the scriptural texts, the sacrament of matrimony, and his knowledge of your relationship. In most situations the presider actually reads aloud your two creations, inserting them between his introductory remarks and concluding observations.

During the last six years I have offered this possibility to more than three hundred engaged couples. About seventy-five percent accepted the invitation. The results, in a wide variety of circumstances, have been overwhelmingly positive. After the wedding I return the original versions to the newly married couple, keeping copies as samples for future couples.

Glen and Mary Manglapus were one such couple. They wrote their own hopes and expectations for their wedding two years ago. I recently asked these young people, both graduate students, to read through my folder full of several hundred versions that had accumulated since the idea's inception. They chose about a dozen that exemplified rather well the basic concept, while still reflecting a diverse number of styles. Their selections form the heart of this publication.

As you will see, there are many ways to go about this. Some people write letters, some write about a particular moment that captures their hopes and dreams, and some even write a poem. What all of these examples have in common is that they are written from the heart, and that's the only important thing. You don't have to be a great writer to express something personal to the one you love, you just have to be yourself.

I am extremely grateful to Mary and Glen for their essential assistance and also to the original writers for their willingness to adopt such an option and their permission to use them in this book. I hope that *From the Heart* will encourage engaged couples in the days ahead to write their own hopes and expectations. May their sharing of these compositions with a presiding clergyman and his sharing of those words with the assembled guests lead to the rich kind of experience that occurred at Glen and Mary's own nuptials.

Part II
Samples of Actual Hopes and Expectations

These hopes and expectations came from the hearts, heads, and hands of couples who have married within the past ten years. While they approved the use of their letter-like compositions, I have altered their names and a few details to shield their identity and preserve their privacy.

1

Sharing

M illions of Americans have read Stephen Covey's *Seven Habits of Highly Effective People*. With an MBA from Harvard and a doctorate from Brigham Young University, as well as being a married man and the father of nine children, he speaks from knowledge and experience about leadership issues in life.

Habit Two states: "Begin with the End in Mind."[1] Start a venture with the goal in view. Have a vision of what you wish to achieve.

When you walk down the aisle for the first time as husband and wife, leaving the church to face the future, we hope that your own end, goal, or vision is to be one.

Oneness is an ideal that we constantly strive for in this life, not an objective we ultimately reach and then relish. There are moments when we do experience a deep sense of being one with each other, but those fleeting events are meant more to encourage us in this journey toward oneness, rather than to indicate that we have attained the desired end.

Still, sharing with each other, being one, has two effects: it doubles our joys and it halves our sorrows.

A mother, reflecting on that truth, made this practical observation and offered some useful advice on the eve of her daughter's wedding: "Cherish the good times and stand by each other in the bad."

Patrick has come to understand the meaning of such sharing and the oneness that results from it. While he had pondered his own hopes and expectations for weeks, Pat wrote the words which follow only hours before the church celebration. That makes them all the more remarkable.

On one of our first dinner dates, Christine reassured me that her eating off my plate was really for the purpose of teaching me to share. Sounds innocent enough, but having grown up with four brothers I was used to protecting food on my plate and not letting someone take from it.

Although Chris knew I was not keen on the idea of her eating off my plate, she continued to do so. In the beginning of our relationship I tried many counterattacks. For example, I tried to barricade my plate with water glasses, bottles, and the salt and pepper shaker—but that didn't work. Chris could retrieve the smallest morsel of food from my plate—skillfully and without a blink of the eye.

One time I got so bothered when Christine ate off my plate that I abruptly asked her to stop. Later, I thought about how quiet she was on the ride home and knew that I had hurt her.

Several weeks later I was having dinner alone on a business trip and I watched an older couple sitting at a nearby table. After they had been served their meals I observed the woman start to reach across the table with fork in hand. At the same moment I watched the man pick up his plate and extend it outward so that his wife would have a smaller reach. "Wow!" I thought to myself. Now that was sharing.

Later that night I thought about the older couple having dinner. I thought about Christine and all the great things that she had already done for me. I realized how much I missed her eating off my plate. She really was teaching me to share. And at that moment, I started to hope.

I hoped that Chris would be eating from my plate the next time I was with her.

I hoped that Chris would be eating from my plate the night I asked her to marry me.

I hoped that Chris would be eating from my plate when we sat down to discuss our wedding plans.

I hoped that Chris would be eating from my plate the evening of our first anniversary, and on the evenings of our second, twenty-fifth, and fiftieth anniversaries.

I hoped that Chris would be eating from my plate the evening she tells me we are having a baby.

I hoped that Chris would be eating from my plate the evening we bring our first baby home.

I hoped that Chris would be eating from my plate the evening we have dinner for our parents in our first house.

I hoped that Chris would be eating from my plate the evenings when she feels sad or low.

I hoped that Chris would be eating from my plate the evenings that I tell her how much I love her and need her.

I hope that Chris will be eating from my plate for years to come—because this will mean that we are together.

I thank God every day for giving me a life with Christine. She has shown me true love. Chris is my miracle.

I hope that she always has peace.

2

Adjusting

Times have changed. When I officiated at marriages in the 50s and 60s, seldom was either the bride or groom a divorced person. Even more rare was the presence in the wedding party of a child or children from previous marriages.

Today those are frequent occurrences.

Many factors have contributed to that change, such as a much higher divorce rate, an altered Catholic church annulment process, and a shift in contemporary attitudes toward these situations.

Marriage will always require adjustments on the part of the new husband and wife. But when one or both have previously married, the adjusting needed will be greater. And when one or both have children from previous relationships, those necessary adjustments will be even greater yet.

Divorce is, in some ways, a much more difficult experience than the death of one we love. The divorced person usually encounters some self-doubt, rejection and self-recrimination, despite the fact that these sentiments are most often unfounded. Moreover, experts in this field indicate that it takes several years for a person to work through the denial, anger, and sadness generally connected with a marital disruption. Furthermore, when a child or children form part of the new mix of relationships, the adjusting becomes more complicated.

During the sign of peace at a recent wedding I observed in particular the groom's two younger children from a previous marriage. They clung tightly to him throughout that part of the ceremony. Watching this scene and noting such conflictual feelings, I pondered how difficult the adjustments in their new home would be and wondered how well they will be made.

Anthony and Mary, as these letters attest, understood those complexities when they first met and adjusted to them later when they married.

Mary,

Well it's been four years and almost three months since we first met and here we are at the altar exchanging vows to be husband and wife. I can't begin to tell you how special this day is for me. In this marriage I not only become a husband, I also become a father to two beautiful kids, Joseph and Nancy. As a family I'm sure we'll be able to handle whatever life has to offer us. So, as a husband and a father, I vow to do my very best in these roles. I think it is very important that we keep an open line of communication between one another, for I think communication is one of the most important aspects in a relationship after love. I really appreciate the way you have brought up your children, and I hope I can be as effective in helping you from this day on. I look forward to the challenge of being your husband and a father.

I would just like to thank your family and friends for making you the person that you are today. Seeing how supportive and caring they are makes me proud to be able to marry into such a beautiful family. I'd like to thank them for all their support in the past and am sure they will be there for us in the future.

Now for my family. I wish I could express my feelings to each individual, but that would be impossible. Therefore, I just want to thank you for all the special things you've done for me in the past. Just knowing that you are all there when I (we) need you takes a huge load off of my (our) shoulders. I thank all of my friends as well for their support and helping me become the person I am today. Mary, I'm sure I speak for all of my family when I say: "Welcome into our family."

There is one special person who will not be with us at this special celebration. But I'm sure she will be watching us from up above. That's my mom. Mom and all of the others who have passed before us in our families, I hope you will watch over us all until some day we will meet again.

Well I guess I've said enough, so Mary as we begin our lives to-gether, let me tell you I love you with all my heart and look forward to spending the rest of my life with you and with your children Joseph and Nancy.

—Love, Anthony

I met Anthony four years ago at a friend's birthday get-together. I never expected to meet anyone there, but we were introduced and have been together ever since.

I told Anthony right away that I was divorced and had two chil-dren. Anthony didn't seem to mind. He immediately forged a bond with Nancy and Joseph. He took them places, played ball, did all the things a father does. He seemed like a natural father!

I also knew right away how special Anthony was. He was funny, caring, sincere, and just a great guy.

Our families are both very close to us. We do things with my family and with his. And always, always, we have a great time. My parents and Anthony's dad have instilled qualities in us that we will in turn pass on to Joseph and Nancy.

I hope we will always love each other as much as we do today.

I hope we will always laugh with and at each other.

I hope "our" children stay healthy and bring us joy.

I expect that we will argue, but I also expect we will come to an agreement on what we argued about. I look forward to spending the rest of my life with Anthony.

3

Befriending

When an engaged couple first meets with me to arrange their wedding, I have some ice-breaking questions that tend to reduce any anxiety they may feel at the outset. Those inquiries also provide interesting background data about the future bride and groom. This information helps us to interact better during the interview and proves very useful later on when I prepare the homily for their nuptial service.

"Where do you work?"

"How did you meet?"

"What were your first impressions of each other?"

"When did you become left-handed (engaged)?"

"Where did he propose and give you the ring?

Those are relatively neutral, nonthreatening questions, yet inquiries that generate easy conversation and much data.

After this relaxed and relaxing discussion comes the first of several challenging questions.

"So you wish to marry. . . . Why him?" And, after her response, "Why her?"

That "Why him?" produces a pause, but soon an often tender exchange occurs. These days the most common response I hear is, "He is my best friend. I can be myself in his presence. When things are bad, he is the first person I call; when something good happens, I want to share it with him. He is always there for me."

Her engaged partner's comments frequently parallel those remarks.

Being each other's best friend is a very sound and excellent basis for building and sustaining a long and successful marital relationship.

Nicholas obviously thinks so. His hopes and expectations took the form of a poem linking together a friend and a wife. His bride, Diana, without naming friendship, details its practical realities.

I've often wished to have a friend
With whom my choicest hours to spend.
To whom I safely might impart
Each wish and weakness of my heart.
Who would in every sorrow cheer
And mingle with my grief a tear.
And to secure that bliss for life,
I'd like that friend to be my wife.

Nicholas,

As we begin our married life together, I can't help but think back over the past six years—the good times and the bad have all been richer being spent with you. You make my life complete, and I can't ever imagine being without you. I love the time we spend together because regardless of what we're doing, together it always seems like fun. You make the tough days easier and the good days more beautiful. Thank you for being the person that you are—the person I love to joke with and enjoy, the person I love to talk seriously with, and the person I love just to be around. I love you with all of my heart.

—Diana

FROM THE HEART

4

Communicating

I know a dynamic and popular keynote speaker at a pre-Cana afternoon regularly begins his remarks with an arresting prediction. It goes something like this:

"All you guys and gals, I am drawing an invisible line down the middle of this group, thus dividing you in two roughly equal sections. Based on current statistics, half of you will see your marriages fail and half of you will see your marriages succeed."

That stuns, sobers, and silences the audience. But the lecturer, a psychologist and well-regarded therapist, then offers the engaged a hopeful projection:

"Here is a promise and a prediction. If you spend five minutes every day talking with each other, truly communicating, your marriage will be a success."

Those who prepare couples for marriage through any of the typical programs today—Engaged Encounter, Pre-Cana Days, One-to-One Sessions—would undoubtedly agree. Communication is the key to marital satisfaction.

Communication is listening with love to the other on a daily basis.

Jean has experienced the hurts that accompany divorce; so has her fiancé, Chuck. But she feels confident about their future together because of the communication factor.

Dear Chuck,

You and I have both been through traumatic times in the past, due to the divorces we've been through. We know so much more now and are wiser. We know each other very well. I expect this marriage will be wonderful because we know how to communicate. We are able to talk about every situation and the problems that arise. We cope very well with the day-to-day stress. Chuck, you are such a wonderful person. Your patience and kind words are never-ending. You would do anything to please me. We both have very difficult situations to contend with—having four children. But I feel we are prepared to handle whatever comes our way. We are together and that's what really matters. Life is so short. I never want to argue about small matters. I want to make every moment with you a good one because you never know what the next day brings. I love you very much, Chuck, and I always will love you.

—Love, Jean

5

Forgiving

Some years ago Judith Viorst wrote a popular book called *Necessary Losses*. It bore this lengthy subtitle: "The loves, illusions, dependencies and impossible expectations that all of us have to give up in order to grow."

We grow, she maintains, by "losing and leaving and letting go."

Those necessary losses include the letting go of expectations for a perfect world and, consequently, a perfect marriage. That means accepting in ourselves and in other people "the mingling of love with hate, of the good with the bad." It means recognizing that there are "flaws in every human connection."[2]

You probably recall those first occasions when you felt totally open and trusting with each other. There were seemingly no barriers, no hiding of your weaknesses, your shadows, your fears. That makes for great closeness, but it also leaves you very vulnerable.

No one can hurt another person as easily and deeply as lovers, as spouses can and do.

But a swiftness to ask for forgiveness and to forgive heals the wound and leaves your love different, but deeper.

Kerry alludes to that imperfection in all relationships and the need for an understanding forgiveness as she writes to her groom-to-be, Norman.

My Dear Norman,

My hopes and expectations for us in our marriage are that we will always remember what brought us to stand before God, our family, and friends today. Our love is our strength. I hope we will always fall back on that love and try to be understanding of each other when we are less than perfect.

I hope we will always look toward God—in joyful times like today, but also in less happy times.

My search for the one person to love and be loved by ended when I met you. Now I expect we will grow and learn together for many long years to come.

All of my love,
—Kerry

6
Discerning

Couples may squirm uneasily when asked where they first met. My immediate follow-up comment generally eases their uncomfortableness and usually produces a chuckle or nod of agreement.

"I know that you will tell your children about how you first met at a church picnic, but the fact is you probably initially connected at Clark's Ale House or Mulrooneys or one of those 'spiritual renewal centers' on Armory Square."

Few actually met at church picnics; others did first connect at a local pub; most, however, became acquainted quite coincidentally at a party, through work, or during some particular celebration like a wedding or graduation.

Coincidence is the key word in these encounters.

In his curious but long-term best-selling novel, *The Celestine Prophecy*, the author describes a mythical search in South America for a series of insights about human existence. The First Insight "occurs when we become conscious of the coincidences in our lives."

These coincidences "strike us as beyond what could be expected by pure chance." We feel "destined, as though our lives had been guided by some unexplained force. The experience induces a feeling of mystery and excitement and, as a result, we feel much alive.

"The First Insight is a reconsideration of the inherent mystery that surrounds our individual lives on this planet."[3]

Most engaged couples I have known would readily apply that novel's words about coincidences to their own initial connection and subsequent courtship. It was not pure chance, but a matter of mystery, of an unexplained force guiding their destiny.

In more traditional Catholic religious terms, we would label their first meeting and later development of the relationship as transcendent events, part of God's mysterious plan for us, a sign of the Lord's special love, an indication of the Creator's divine protective providence working in our lives.

Eugene injected those thoughts about discerning God's mysterious ways into his own hopes and expectations for his approaching marriage with Roberta.

I remember a conversation with my mother when I was about nine years old. I asked her, "How do you know when you meet the person that you will marry?" She gave me a typical motherly answer like, "Something inside you will tell you." Then my follow-up question was, "Suppose the girl who is right for me lives far away like in New York. How will I ever meet her?" Mom again replied, "If she is the one that is right for you, God will have your paths cross to allow you to meet her." Well when I met Roberta we were balancing beer glasses on each other's heads. I guess the Lord does work in mysterious ways.

Once we met, we began to see a lot of each other and the relationship moved at a rather rapid pace, because it felt so comfortable. Similar personalities, backgrounds, and interests furthered my interest in Roberta. I had never found someone with whom I could just be myself without putting up some kind of false impression. There is nothing we can't say, talk about, or do in front of each other. We laugh a lot. Sometimes there are tears, but knowing that we have the loving support of each other always makes it easier to overcome them. Roberta is my best friend.

Our love for each other grew to the point where I considered proposing marriage to her. It was the easiest decision I have ever made. (Some say it will be the last decision I ever make too.) We are a good team and enjoy going through the good times and bad times together. We certainly have had our share of both lately.

I really do not have any grand illusions of what marriage will bring except a continuance of what we have now. I am very satisfied with our relationship and would never want Roberta to change for me. I love her for who she is today. And as time always brings us change, I feel confident that we will adapt to whatever we are confronted with and continue on with our lives.

I do not view this marriage as starting a new family, but extending my existing family to include Roberta's. I am very proud to welcome such a good, loving family into my own.

7

Begetting

Whenever I preside at a baptism, I encourage parents to recall the moment of their baby's birth. How did they feel at that instant when their child, the singular fruit of their love, came forth into this world? What were their feelings during those minutes immediately afterward?

Words like these regularly surface: grateful, overwhelmed, incredible, filled with joy, proud, a miracle.

A now retired obstetrician often remarked that despite delivering thousands of babies, he never ceased to marvel at the experience, the miracle of it all. The new catechism provides a theological basis for this sense of wonderment and the miracle surrounding every birth experience. It states that God directly creates each human soul, that immaterial, spiritual, and thus immortal principle of life.

Consequently, we can say that three forces or, better, persons enter into the conception process: the father, the mother, and God.

John's letter to Doreen takes the form of a poem and includes his dreams of miraculously begetting children with her, special persons that only the two of them, working with the Lord, could produce.

Dear Doreen,
I can't wait to see you
                walking down the aisle.
I can't wait to see you
                glowing with a smile.
I can't wait to see you
                in your silky white gown.
I can't wait to see you
                when you come walking down.
I can't wait to see us
                walking out side by side.
I can't wait to see us
                on our limousine ride.
I can't wait to see us
                holding each other tight.
I can't wait to see us
                going on without fright.
I can't wait to see them
                whether it's one or two.
I can't wait to see them
                if it's pink or blue.
I can't wait to see them
                playing with their toys.
I can't wait to see them,
                laughing and giggling with joy.
I can't wait to see us
                when we're old and gray.
I can't wait to see us
                as we sit and rock all day.
                Doreen, I love you.
                    — John

                        FROM THE HEART

8

Rejoicing

Some couples travel a distance to celebrate their nuptials in the California wine country of Napa Valley. Some citizens of Copenhagen opt for their weddings in a centuries-old church of that city. Some engaged people in Japan seek to marry within a Catholic chapel even though they are not Roman Catholics.

There is a common word or thread linking these three situations: beauty. The California countryside is beautiful; so, too, is the venerable structure in Copenhagen; and the Japanese prefer church buildings of beauty rather than plain governmental offices for their marital vows.

Author, psychologist, and therapist Thomas Moore observes in his popular book *Care of the Soul* that "beauty is arresting." It lifts us from the rush of practical life into "the contemplation of timeless and eternal realities."[4]

To put this another way, something beautiful—a sunrise or sunset, a ring or dress, a church interior or wedding service—can take us from the ordinary to the transcendent, from the here and now to the hereafter, from the human to the divine. Beauty has the power to connect us with God.

Beauty causes us to rejoice, to experience an inner peace and happiness. It is little wonder, then, that couples seek to surround their marriage celebration with beauty, to include a variety of beautiful elements in their nuptial service.

Patricia, with her letter, and Mark, with his poetry, capture some of those sentiments about joy and happiness, sunsets and sunrises, music and marriage, as they express their hopes and expectations.

Dear Mark,

Well, the time has come. We're finally getting married. I've waited a long time for this. Our wedding day will be the happiest day of my life. I was shocked and delighted the day you asked me to marry you. Tears come to my eyes when I think of or listen to the song you wrote for me. It is so special and meaningful. (And I know what you're thinking—everything makes me cry, but the song meant a great deal to me.) The happiest day of my life before this was the first time you told me you loved me. I will always cherish that moment.

Who would have thought all those years ago when you were stepping on my toes at the band banquet that we'd someday end up married. We have grown up together, and I am so happy to have reached this point with you. I've loved you for a very long time, and I am so happy and proud to become your wife. I look forward to having children with you and spending the rest of our lives together.

I love that you are my friend, that you make me laugh, that in good times and bad you have always been there for me. I will always love you for comforting me when my mother died. You were the strength that helped me through it. It meant the world to me. You've always been there for me in times of trouble, no matter what the state of our relationship. You've supported my career decisions and the other important decisions I have had to make. Even when we weren't "going out," I always knew I could count on your friendship and support.

We've had our ups and downs, but in the end it's always been us. I love you so much. I couldn't live without you. We've had so many good times together, I look forward to continuing them into our old age. I am happy to know that you will always be around to make me laugh or comfort me during sad times. Please know that I am always here for you too.

FROM THE HEART

Thank you for putting up with me through the years. I know some of my habits drive you crazy. I truly appreciate your loving me through and in spite of my faults. I can't wait to walk down the aisle and marry you!!!

Love always,
——Patricia

Patricia,

I hope I'm there to praise you——at times when you achieve.

I hope I'm always with you——when it's time to leave.

I hope I'm there to comfort——when you feel pain.

I hope I'm there with shelter——when it starts to rain.

I hope I'm there with answers——when questions do arise.

I hope that every sunset——is followed by sunrise.

I hope that when you feel hunger——I can provide you with some food.

I hope that when you're angry——I'm there to change your mood.

I hope that when you're at a loss——I'm there to help you seek.

I hope I'm there to offer strength——when you feel weak.

I hope that when you feel sad——I can make you laugh.

I hope you win the lottery——so you can give me half.

I hope that when you start to cry——I'm there to wipe the tear.

I hope I can protect you——from everything you fear.

I hope I'll always be there——when you need me to.

I hope you always remember——that I truly do love you.

——Mark

Rejoicing

9
Believing

Over the past two decades, without much prompting from anyone, a great number, perhaps a majority of couples, have incorporated the unity candle within their nuptial service.

It is purely an option, not something required by church worship regulations. Moreover, the kind of candle used, where the lighting occurs in the ceremony, and how this transpires varies with each bride and groom.

We could draw out a dozen connections between this burning wedding candle and the spiritual dimensions of marriage. However, probably the most obvious connection centers around Jesus Christ, the light of the world.

It was the risen Christ who first came into the hearts of the bride and/or groom at baptism, a presence symbolized then by a personalized baptismal candle lighted from the large Easter or paschal candle.

It was the risen Christ who worked his first miracle at a wedding in Cana of Galilee, where he changed water into wine during the festive reception.

It was the risen Christ who in his loving providence brought together the couple now marrying before the altar.

It is the risen Christ who cements their relationship during the exchange of vows and binds them as one for life.

It is the risen Christ who in the sacrament of matrimony assures the spouses that he will remain with them all the days of their lives.

It is the risen Christ who promises to be by their side always, especially in periods of darkness and difficulty.

Jesus urges the couple in such troublesome moments: "Turn to me and my gentle, but powerful light will guide your journeys and strengthen your hearts."

Maureen believes in God and in Jesus Christ, the light of the world. That faith permeates her letter to Andrew, an equally strong believer in the Lord.

Dear Andrew,

My expectations and hopes for our marriage are quite simple. It's to have a triumphant marriage! That's the kind of relationship my parents have. I've always admired my parents' relationship. They are still passionately in love. The tenderness, love, and affection they display for each other is so beautiful. My parents have a deep adoration for each other and have been totally committed to serving each other and their family.

That's what I hope to do for you, Andrew. We have what my parents have——unconditional love and total devotion to each other. God has brought us together to serve each other. God has blessed me with my parents because they taught me what love is. I have waited a long time to give my love to a quality man, a man like my father. My parents have been my role models. I've always wanted nothing less than the kind of

marriage they have——a triumphant one, a godly one. God
has blessed my parents with a beautiful, loving, healthy,
happy family——a family full of love, kindness, support, en-
couragement, and patience. This is the kind of family I dream
of for us. I'm sure we will have our share of tough times; let's
face it, life is stressful.

Our friend's grandfather said, "The road to a happy marriage is always under construction." This is so true. Our love
will not be taken for granted or neglected, but nurtured and
cared for all the days of our lives. God will be in the center
of our world holding us together. With his love we have nothing to fear. Our love will endure all. And only in the end can
we say our marriage has been a triumphant one, a passionate
one, the one I've always dreamed of with you.

All my love,
——Maureen

Part III
A Word for the Presiding Clergy

At clergy conferences on the pastoral dimensions of marriage, I frequently take an on-the-spot survey of participants. Having elicited from them an agreement to raise their hands immediately if the answer to the inquiry is affirmative, I pose this question: "How many of you in the relatively recent past have celebrated a nuptial service and, afterward, been told by a family member or guest that this was the most beautiful wedding ceremony that they have ever attended?"

Without fail, every priest or deacon present instantly lifts his hand.

If we were to pursue this issue with the affirming family members or guests and seek to identify the reason for such praise, they probably would respond, "It was so personal."

A personalized nuptial service can, of course, mean many things. Yet at the very least the remark indicates that the presider made the celebration special for the couple, that he seemingly knew them, that the priest or deacon included elements which were unique to the bride and groom.

Videotaping weddings performed by a dozen clergy, including their homilies, and then viewing them together at one time would be a fascinating experience. We all possess quite different styles. Moreover, each of us has developed over the years a homily or homilies with phrases and examples that apparently work, that touch not only the bride and groom, but also the assembled guests. We have grown rather comfortable and confident with the basic material.

A problem occurs, however, when you officiate at many weddings for several years in the same parish. You begin to feel awkward knowing that a good number of those present, even the bride and groom, are familiar with your favorite thoughts or illustrations, however valid and potent.

That challenge accidentally spawned the idea of *From the Heart.* I had been presiding at fifty to sixty nuptials annually for a few years at the same church and started to feel this uneasiness. At first I contemplated composing a half dozen nuptial homilies during the generally non-marriage winter months. That would provide a greater variety of thoughts for me to integrate with the readings and the couple's background throughout the wedding season.

I never did accomplish this task. In fact, I never developed even one.

Then somehow, from somewhere, perhaps through one of those gentle inspirations of the Holy Spirit, the idea of encouraging the couple to write their hopes and expectations entered my mind. The results were an immediate success: the couples enjoyed writing their remarks, the family and guests invariably were deeply moved when they heard these very personal sharings, and I had an element that made my preparation easier and homilies fresher.

In my sequence of marriage preparation I spend two hours with the couple when they first arrange the wedding date. That period of time allows for personal interchange, an explanation of the standard nuptial necessities (documents, music, *Together for Life,* a variety of pre-Cana options, rehearsal date, etc.), viewing of my thirty-minute video *We Want to Get Married* (Tabor), and their completion of FOCUS, the premarital inventory.

Upon departure they understand that we need to get together again for an hour about two months prior to the wedding. During this later session we review their preparation, answer questions about the actual ceremony, and complete prenuptial paperwork. It is then that I describe and offer to them the option of writing their hopes and expectations.

While one sits with me as we complete the investigation document, the other reads through the folder containing hopes and expectations compiled by earlier couples. They then exchange places, and we repeat the procedure.

Before leaving I remind them to bring the license, the *Together for Life* tear-out sheet, the offering envelope, and their hopes and expectations to the rehearsal. As Part I noted, about seventy-five percent select this alternative and almost all agree to have me use their composition as part of the ceremony.

It is relatively easy to merge into a homily their choice of the scriptural readings, a fundamental message on matrimony, their hopes and expectations, and one's knowledge of the couple.

After the ceremony I return the original version to them either through one of the attendants or later by mail. A copy goes into my folder for future use.

After this booklet has been published I will continue to have the couples read through the contents of that folder at the session described. They thus can see those letters in their original form. However, I will now, in addition, give them a copy of this publication to take home for further guidance.

How does this concept mesh with liturgical norms governing the nature of the homily? I see no conflict; in fact, the option even fulfills various ideals mentioned in official documents.

The General Instruction of the Roman Missal states that the content of the homily ideally "should be an exposition of the scripture readings or of some particular aspect of them, or of some other text taken from the Order or the Proper of the Mass for the day, having regard for the mystery being celebrated or the special needs of those who hear it."[5]

The introduction to the *Rite of Marriage* notes that the homilist "should relate his instructions to the texts of the sacred readings." Later it recommends that priests and deacons "show special consideration to those who take part in liturgical celebrations or hear the gospel only on the occasion of a wedding, either because they are not Catholics, or because they are Catholics who rarely, if ever, take part in the eucharist or seem to have abandoned the practice of their faith. Priests are ministers of Christ's gospel to everyone."[6]

Some time ago nationally known lecturer and author, pastor and preacher, Father Frank McNulty of New Jersey codirected a parish mission for me at St. Joseph's Church in Camillus, New York. During his visit, as we discussed various pastoral matters, I mentioned the hopes and expectations alternative.

Several years later, in a letter just prior to his retirement as pastor, he told of adopting the option with his own couples and for his own homilies at weddings. The idea, Father McNulty commented, was "pure gold." I pray that many other priests and deacons will likewise find this creative and personalizing feature golden for them as well.

Notes

1. Stephen Covey, *The Seven Habits of Highly Effective People* (New York: Simon and Schuster, 1989), Habit 2, pp. 95-144.

2. Judith Viorst, *Necessary Losses* (New York: Fawcett Gold Medal, 1986), pp. 2-3.

3. James Redfield, *The Celestine Prophecy* (New York: Time Warner Company, 1993), pp. 6-7.

4. Thomas Moore, *Care of the Soul* (New York: HarperCollins Publishers, 1992), pp. 278-279.

5. *The Rites*, "General Instruction of the Roman Missal" (New York: Pueblo Publishing Company, 1976), Article 41, pp. 172-173.

6. Ibid., "Introduction" for *Rite of Marriage*, Article 9, p. 536.

Your Thoughts

Your Thoughts

Father Joseph M. Champlin currently serves as rector at the Cathedral of the Immaculate Conception in his home diocese of Syracuse, New York. In his forty-three years of priesthood he has presided at thousands of marriages and is the author of *Together for Life*, the most popular marriage preparation booklet in the U.S. for over twenty-five years.

He has traveled more than two million miles lecturing here and abroad on pastoral subjects and has written forty-two books. His most recent works include *The Marginal Catholic, Through Death to Life, What It Means to Be Catholic, The Visionary Leader, With Hearts Light as Feathers, A Thoughtful Word, A Healing Touch, Why Go to Confession?* and *Father Champlin on Contemporary Issues: The Ten Commandments and Today's Catholics.*

Keeping a wedding homily fresh is always a challenge. So is the task of relating it to the lives of the couple. That's why priests and deacons will find *From the Heart* an invaluable resource for crafting homilies that not only reflect the readings and the Church's vision of marriage, but provide a sure way to speak personally to the couples and to their assembled families and friends.

Fr. Joseph Champlin, author of *Together for Life* and a noted speaker on marriage preparation and the *Rite of Marriage*, has developed this simple way to incorporate the couple's hopes and expectations for the marriage. They do so separately and without showing those compositions to one another. At the rehearsal, they present these to the priest or deacon. He in turn weaves their words into his homily, blending their thoughts with his own reflections on the scriptural texts and the sacrament of matrimony.

From the Heart provides a convenient way to introduce this practice into your ministry. Designed as a companion to *Together for Life*, it can be given to the couple as a guidebook to use in their own writing. It provides a simple, clear explanation of the practice and offers samples of how nine couples actually used this approach. Their personal reflections, letters, poems provide models to spur the imaginations of the engaged couple. In addition, each of the nine reflections is preceded by remarks from the author. Thus *From the Heart* is not only a tool for homily preparation, but another valuable resource to use in marriage preparation.

Discover for yourself how easy and practical this approach is. As Fr. Champlin notes: "The couples have enjoyed writing their remarks and their families and guests invariably have been deeply moved. It makes my preparation easier and my homilies fresher."